# Contents

Contents
Introduction
Empanada dough
Baking empanadas
Empanada dough for use in baking
Simple fillings for baked empanada
Using small 10cm empanada discs
Using larger 16cm empanada discs
Baking the empanada
Flakier and tastier empanada dough
Sweet empanada dough for baking
Fried empanada
Empanada dough for use in frying

Sweet empanada dough for frying
Empanada for frying made from Masa harina
Frying the empanada
Empanada recipes from around the world
Argentina
  Beef empanadas
Belize
  Fish panada
Columbia
  Pork and beef empanada
Chile
  Pino empanada
Indian
  Samosa
Great Britain
  Cornish Pasty
Conclusion

# Introduction

Empanada is a Spanish word which is essentially used to describe food covered or wrapped in bread. Although this is the original meaning, these days, it covers breads that have been stuffed with fillings as well as those enclosed in pastry. These foods are then either baked or fried. They are eaten a lot in Spain and also in Central and Southern America.

This is not to say that other countries don't have their own versions of this type of food. In none Spanish speaking countries they also occur but are known by a variety of different names. In the UK people are used to calling them pasties, turnovers or even hand pies. Likewise in India the Samosa is a fried kind of empanada. Empanadas across the world look different and taste different. As a result there are numerous different recipes to try out, each reflecting the tastes of a particular part of the world. An example of this is the Cornish pasty from the UK. The pasty is a regional delicacy made in the Cornwall region. The Cornish pasty has a particular type of filling and design that makes it very recognisable as well as a special history related to Cornish mineworkers. Wherever you go you will find some type of local Empanada and they are all worth finding out about and trying.

The beauty of the empanada is that there are huge number of different fillings that can be added. Indeed, you can make up your own special fillings so that you put your own mark on what you produce. In this way making empanada is a very creative enterprise. You can also use them as a very delicious way to use up leftovers that would otherwise end up being thrown away. The humble empanada can easily expand the basic range of meals that you can produce and is also very useful if you just want to have something a little bit different from time to time.

## Empanada dough

Making dough for empanadas is quite easy. With a food processor you can whiz it up really quickly. However, it is also easy enough to make it by hand. This is because the dough only needs a small amount of kneading. In fact, it is best not to overwork the dough, which means you actually stand to make better dough by using your hands!

The dough is rolled out a cut to form discs which are then used to make individual empanada. These discs can be bought ready made in frozen form from food stores, that either specialise in Latin American food or have a section dedicated to it. These readymade discs are in actual fact rather good, but in the end homemade ones will always be better. When you make your own dough you are in control of the quality of the ingredients used and you can make sure that they are the best. In particular, commercial producers may use lower quality fats to reduce cost and will also use additives such as preservatives and flavour enhancers. If you care about these things make your own. Besides fresh homemade discs always taste fresher and better. One more great thing about homemade dough is that you can add herbs and spices which will improve flavours and enhance the taste of the fillings that you decide to use.

When making a new batch of empanada dough it is a good idea to keep in mind that if you make a large amount of it you can easily freeze the remaining discs for use at a later date. The best way to do this is to roll out the discs and then freeze them in stacks of useful numbers. You need to separate out each disc in the stack and the best way to do this is to used waxed paper. In this way the discs can more easily be separated out, when they need to be used and they won't just fuse into an awkward lump when they are defrosted.

The dough used for baking and frying is subtly different due to the way each method of cooking reacts with it. It is therefore best to keep in mind your eventually method of cooking before producing the dough. Some types of empanada such as the Indian samosa are designed to be fried whereas the Cornish pasty is designed to be baked. Here are the basic recipes for each type:

# Baking empanadas

Baking is probably the most popular way of cooking empanadas. All you need is a decent oven and some baking trays or sheets.

## Empanada dough for use in baking

**Ingredients**

375g plain flour
150g refrigerated salted butter

1 medium sized slightly whisked egg
60ml to 100ml cold water

**Method**

Prepare the chilled butter by cutting it into cubes. If you want more control over the salt content of the dough you can use unsalted butter and then add salt up to about a ¼ tsp of salt to taste.

It is important to keep things cool when making this dough. Don't let the butter melt. If necessary keep the cubes of butter in the fridge until they are needed. The water should be cold enough from the tap so long as it has been run for a while. If you are unsure, put the water in the fridge for a while before using it. Although you can make this butter based dough using a food processor it is best to make it by hand. It doesn't take long to make it by hand and has the benefit of producing less things that to have to wash up at the end. In addition to this, a food processor breaks up the butter too much, and this means that the empanada pie crust won't be as crisp or flaky as the handmade version.

**1 Using a food processor:**

Put the plain four into the bowl of the processor and then add the butter cubes, egg and 60ml of water. Whizz up the mixture until the dough joins together in a rough ball. If needed, add extra water a little at a time until the dough clumps together. Be careful not to add too much water. Try not to over work the dough

**2 By hand:**

Put the plain flour into a large mixing bowl and then add the cubes of butter.

Separate out the cubes of butter by using your hands to mix them into the flour.

Use a pastry blender to cut the butter into the flour.

Continue cutting the butter into the flour until the butter is in pea sized lumps.

add the egg and use a rubber spatula or your hands to mix everything together.

Slowly add the water and continue to mix until the dough comes together in a ball. Try not to add too much water but if it does get too sticky you can always add a little flour to the outside of the ball until it can easily be handled.

Take the dough ball, from which ever method you have used, and flatten it slightly into a thick disc. Note that the butter can still be seen as small solid yellow areas within the dough. This is normal and indeed desirable. The reason for this is that these little butter areas make the dough nice and flaky and crispy when the empanadas are cooked.

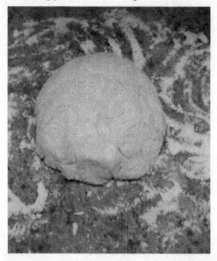

Cover the disc in plastic wrap and the place it in the refrigerator.

Leave it in the fridge for between 1 and 2 hours before you use it.

**Making dough discs**

Once the dough has been cooled take it out of the fridge, unwrap it and place on a floured work surface. Use a rolling pin to roll out the dough into thin sheets about 2 to 3 mm thick. Keep the work surface under the dough floured as you proceed so that the dough doesn't stick to it. Don't roll the dough too thin as it will be difficult to construct the empanada due to breakage. Once the dough is rolled out cut discs out of it using a round mould cutter or a plate and a sharp knife. Traditional empanada discs are about 10 to 14cm in diameter. However, they can be made whatever size that you desire. Larger discs can be stuffed with more filling. Choose the size of plate or mould cutter relative to the size of empanada you want to produce. For smaller empanada you can use a cookie cutter. Use one that is about 10cm or the size of the palm of your hand.

**Cutting 16cm discs with a plate and sharp knife**

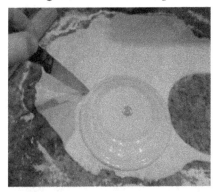

**Making smaller 10cm discs using a cookie cutter**

The dough recipe given above will allow you to produce around 30 of these smaller discs. Roll out the remaining dough and cut further discs until you have used all of the dough up.

**Discs ready for filling**

If you are having trouble rolling and cutting the thin dough used specifically for frying you can try making small balls of dough and then rolling them out individually for each disc. It doesn't really matter if the discs aren't quite round as they will work just the same. You should use the discs once they are freshly made or store them in the fridge or freezer to be used at a later time.

**Putting the empanada together**

You will need a filling of some kind in order to continue. The fillings need to be already cooked. You can't really use uncooked filling especially if they are meat based. See the later sections for fillings that you might choose.

The amount of filling that you use will depend on the size of empanada discs that you have made. Small empanada will only need a spoonful of the filling. The amount of filling that you can use will improve with experience. To start off with, it is best to keep the filling to small amounts so that the construction of the empanada is easier. If you use too much filling for the size of your empanada you will more than likely have problems. These problems include:

*The breakup of the pastry disc as you fold it.*

*Problems sealing the edges of the empanada.*

*The rupture of the empanada during cooking and the release of its contents.*

If you end up having these problems you should first consider reducing the amount of filling that you use. There is a great temptation to try and use up all of the filling that is there and this can lead to overstuffed empanada. With practice you will be able to judge the amount of filling to use and make your empanada so that are well stuffed and not have any problems.

Put a spoonful of the filling in the centre of each of the empanada discs.

Sealing an empanada can be a problem and as a result it can be useful to use a 'glue' at the joint. The best way to glue them together is to use a pastry brush to brush the edges of the disc with whisked egg wash. When the edges are pressed together the egg wash will act as a glue. Another glue that can be used is a thin coating of milk, which can be once again applied using a pastry brush.

Fold the dough disc over the filling and press the dough edges together using your fingers so that a seal is made.

A fork can be used on the seal edge in order to help with sealing, as can pinching with the fingers as you would with a pie crust. Some empanada have folded edges. You can also try this as it helps to seal the empanada as well. In some types of empanada the folding of the seal is part of the design and is done in a special way to produce an identifiable design feature. You can experiment with pinching and folding to produce your own edge designs.

Some designs from Latin American have special names such as the following:

A fork is used to press on the edge join to help seal the empanada. Typically this is done 5 times and is known as the **_Pollo_** design.

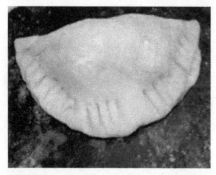

The edge of the empanada is pinched and extended into 5 points. This is known as the **_Humita_** design

The joined edge has been pinched and formed into a wave shape using the fingers. This is known as the **_Cordero_** design.

The pointy ends of the basic empanada can be pulled towards each other until they can be joined to make a design that is just about circular. This is

known as the *Puerro* design.

Some of these designs are more difficult than others and they take practice to achieve well. To start off with, just concentrate on making sure that the seals work without leaking rather than creating a design. Once you have got this right you can experiment with the designs starting with the forking and wavy ones as they are the easiest of the bunch.

Once the empanada have been constructed you can put them in the refrigerator for about a half an hour in order to make the edge seals even stronger before they are cooked.

## Simple fillings for baked empanada

Once you have prepared the dough and cut the discs to the size that you require it is time to think about the fillings. There are 2 strategies that you could use when making a batch of empanada. You could go for producing all of them with the same filling for example you might decide that you just want to make potato and cheese empanada. These are easy to put together as you only need a few ingredients for the filling and stuffing them is a production line of exactly the same processes. The other strategy is to produce a variety of differently filled empanada. This is a little more difficult as you have to make sure that you have a number of different ingredients all available at the same time. Your choice really depends on what you are trying to achieve. If you are just trying to use up leftovers, then the fillings you use will depend upon the leftovers that you have available at the time. If you are trying to put on a show of different tastes for a dinner party, or just have a number of different snacks for the family to be tempted by, you will need to buy in the ingredients specially. As the fillings need to be cooked first it is best to prepare them altogether before you start putting any of the empanada together. If you are making the small 10cm empanada you only need small amounts of the ingredients. The easiest way to cook them is to fry them. Chop up an onion, a mushroom, a green pepper, a couple of chilies, some garlic cloves and anything else you want to include. Put these in a large frying pan with some olive oil. Put them in different areas of the pan so you can remove each group of ingredients when they are cooked.

**Fried red chilies**

**Fried garlic**

**Fried green bell pepper strips**

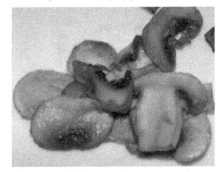

**Fried sliced mushroom**

**Fried chopped onion**

You can also fry a small amount of minced beef or a sausage/sausage meat.

**Fried minced beef**

**Single fried sausage**

You can also boil and mash and single potato and sweet potato and then mash them.

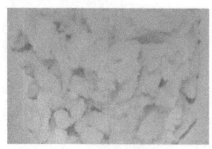

**Mashed potato**

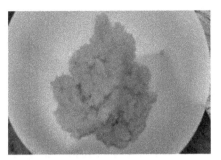

**Mashed sweet potato**

Get together your other ingredients such as grated cheddar cheese, boiled ham, spring onion and whole grain mustard

## Using small 10cm empanada discs

For these smaller 10cm discs the filling should be around the size of a heaped teaspoon. Obviously the amount you can get away with will become more obvious the more empanadas that you try to stuff.

Put the cooked ingredients in the centre and leave a gap round the outside so that the egg wash glue can be applied.

**Minced beef, onion, garlic and chili.**

**Grated cheddar cheese, green olive, garlic and green pepper.**

Ham, mushroom, red chili and garlic.

Ham, whole grain mustard and green spring onion.

Pepperoni and grated Cheddar cheese.

**Mashed potato, grated cheddar cheese, chili, onion and garlic.**

**Half fried Sausage**

Put in the centre of disc and then the dough folded over the sausage until it is enclosed.

Completed sausage empanada or **Choriempa**

**Sweet mashed potato, fried onion, garlic and green spring onion.**

# Using larger 16cm empanada discs

Far more filling can be used in these larger empanada discs. Put the filling in the centre. Leave a free space all around the edge of the disc to apply the egg wash so that a good join can be made. Try not to pile up the filling too high as the disc edges won't meet when you fold them inwards.

**Brie cheese, fried mushroom and green pepper strips.**

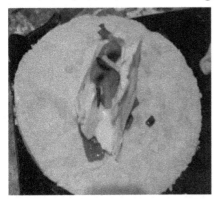

**Grated Cheddar cheese, sun dried tomatoes, and chopped green spring onion.**

**Grated Cheddar cheese and green pesto.**

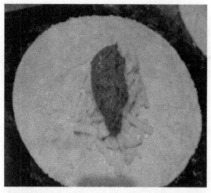

**Hummus, green olives and sun dried tomato**

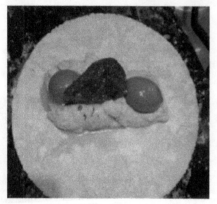

Once you are near the end of the dough and the fillings that you have prepared you can decide to use them up in 1 larger empanada. It doesn't matter that this last one is exactly disc shaped. Just roll out the dough as near as you can and then fill it with the remaining fillings. Just make sure that there is enough room at the edges to apply the egg wash and fold the empanada to join the edges.

**Large irregular last empanada**

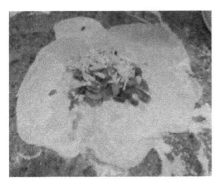

## Baking the empanada

**Place the empanada on a greased baking sheet.**

The empanada can be baked as they are but a pleasant golden brown surface can be achieved by brushing the top surface with an egg wash made by whisking an egg with a tablespoon of water. Milk can also be used but isn't quite as good as using egg.

**16cm empanadas after brushing with egg wash**

Place the empanada into a preheated an oven set to 200C or 400F. The baking time will depend on the size of each empanada. Small ones will take less time to cook. They will be ready once they are golden brown in colour which will be somewhere between 20 and 30 minutes. Smaller empanada tend to cook more quickly and having a fan oven also speeds up the baking time. As a result it is best to keep an eye on how they are progressing from 15 minutes onwards.

**Baked 16cm empanadas with the large irregular bottom left**

**Baked 10cm empanadas**

# Flakier and tastier empanada dough

Butter is the secret to getting flakier, crispier and tastier dough for making empanadas. Butter also makes the dough more resilient and easier to roll and shape. You can therefore try this all butter dough which is normally used for pie pastry crust. This dough is especially good for making larger empanada.

### Ingredients

325g Plain Flour
200g Salted Cold Butter (or use unsalted and add salt to taste)
120 ml Cold Water

60 ml Cold Water

Egg wash

**Method**

Make this in exactly the same way as the above method described for empanada dough except that there is no egg to be added. Cut the discs in the same way or simply roll out to make very large empanada. Brush the surface with egg wash before baking to get a golden colour as it bakes.

When making a large empanada you can make the filling out of large chunky cooked vegetables and meats such as stewing steak. My favourite is to make one from potato, carrot, cheddar cheese and fried bacon bits.

**Large empanada result**

As you can see this cheese and vegetable empanada takes up nearly the whole of the baking sheet. It was made using the full butter dough as described in this section.

# Sweet empanada dough for baking

The doughs described so far are savoury ones. The following dough is sweet. This can be used with sweet fillings or with savoury ones where it produces a nice contrast to the empanada's savoury contents. This dough has less butter and more lard. This results in a less flaky appearance giving a more silky smooth crust that also has the advantage of soaking up liquid content of the fillings used. This dough needs to rest in the fridge overnight so you need to start preparing it the day before.

**Ingredients**

512g plain flour
1 teaspoon salt
2 tablespoon sugar
25g butter, chilled
170g cold lard
180ml to 240ml water
2 egg yolks

**Method**

Pour the flour into a large mixing bowl. Mix in the salt and sugar.

Use a pastry cutter to blend the lard and butter into the dry mixture until everything is blended quite well.

Put the egg yolks and 180ml of water into a small bowl or jug and whisk then to mix. Add the liquid to the dry mixture a little at a time whilst mixing with a rubber spatula. Once the dough starts coming together, knead it and continue adding small amounts of the egg and water mixture. Stop once the dough becomes smooth. Add some of the extra water if needed. The idea is to get a smooth pliable dough and not one that is elastic in nature. If it gets a little too soggy, add some extra flour to the outside until it can be handled. Put the dough in some plastic wrap and place it in the fridge overnight so that it is ready to use the next day.

On the next day place the dough ball on a floured work surface and roll it out to the normal thickness for empanada discs. This amount of dough should make about a dozen largish empanada.

Fruit fillings can be used together with sugar for sweetening any sour fruits such as black currants. Hard fruits such as apples will need to be stewed before they are used in order to soften them. More delicate fruits such as raspberries can be used as they are. Stuff the empanada discs with the fruit and then bake as normal. Serve sweet empanada with cream or custard.

## Fried empanada

Fried empanada have a different flavour and crispy fluffier texture compared to those that are baked. frying is quicker than baking especially if you have a deep fat fryer.

## Empanada dough for use in frying

The dough used for frying is slightly different to that used for baking. One aim is to produce a dough that will puff up during the frying process. The following recipe is designed to do that.

**Ingredients**

350g Plain flour
¼ tsp Salt or to taste
60ml Sunflower oil
130 ml water

**Method**

**1 Using a food processor:**

Add the plain flour and salt to the processor bowl and whizz up briefly to combine them. Add the sunflower oil and half the water to the dry mixture and Whizz up once again. Continue processing as you add the rest of the water until a smooth dough is formed.

Form the dough into a ball and place the dough on a floured work surface and flatten it into a flat disc.

Cover the dough disc in plastic wrap and put into the fridge to cool overnight, or for at least a couple of hours

**2 By hand:**

Add the flour and salt to a large mixing bowl and combine them well. Add the sunflower oil and water to the dry mixture and stir with a wooden spoon or rubber spatula. Tip the stirred mixture onto a floured work surface and then knead it until it becomes smooth. This will take around ten to fifteen minutes working. Roll the smooth dough into a ball and flatten slightly to produce a thick disc. Cover the disc with plastic wrap and place in the refrigerator for at least 2 hours.

After the 2 hours cooling use the methods outlined in the previous section to roll out the empanada dough and cut discs. Empanada fry better if the dough is rolled as thin as you can without it breaking up.

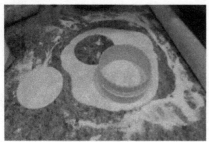

Add the fillings and then fold and seal each empanada.

**Broccoli and Stilton cheese filling before sealing**

Apply an egg wash seal with a brush or use your finger dipped in the egg wash.

**A batch of empanada ready for frying**

To make a dough that has a light and fluffy appearance you can add a teaspoon of baking powder to the recipe. This should be added with the other dry ingredients at the start of the process.

Butter can be used to make frying batter too but you need to reduce the amount to 100g and substitute it for the Sunflower oil in the above recipe.

## Sweet empanada dough for frying

Use the sweet dough recipe given in the baking session but leave out the egg yolks. Follow the same method but roll out the dough a little thinner so that the empanadas will cook better when they are fried.

## Empanada for frying made from Masa

# harina

Masa harina is a type of corn flour that is used in Latin American countries for making empanada and tortilla. It is also called Tortilla flour too. This is a special kind of flour and is not the same as the item we call Corn flour that is used for thickening sauces. You cannot use this kind of corn flour to make empanada. Masa harina is prepared in such a way that it allows a dough to form. The corn goes through a process called nixtamalization which means that when water is added to it the ground up corn tends to stick together forming a dough. In Latina America the making of empanada and tortilla is so popular that you can buy the dough readymade and use it straight away. In other countries, such as the UK, it can be difficult to even find masa harina in the shops, and as a result you may have to order it from a specialist Mexican online store or even from Amazon. It can however be expensive. Maseca is a popular brand of masa harina and one that is used in Mexico. A cheaper alternative that may be available in some supermarkets is this one made by P.A.N.

Follow the instructions given on the pack of flour to make up the dough. Roll the dough into balls about the size of golf balls.

The empanada dough made from PAN isn't as resilient as that from wheat flour and as a result you have to be a little more careful when you are making the discs and stuffing them. In order to stop corn flour discs from sticking to work surfaces and falling apart when handling them there is a special trick involved. The method used is to, roll the discs out between plastic sheets. The plastic sheet used depends on what you have available. Typically in Latin America plastic bags are used. Even shopping bags are often used. You have to cut out pieces of the bag that are a bit larger than the discs you want to make. You should make sure that these bags are clean before you use them. I usually use small sandwich bags that I buy from the supermarket. You can use these without cutting them up. Put one bag on the work surface and place a ball of the dough onto it. Place another bag on top of the dough ball. You can now use a rolling pin to roll out the dough into a disc.

### Rolling a disc between plastic

The whole problem with rolling the disc in this way is that it is often difficult to get the shape right and the edges can end up quite irregular which in turn makes it difficult to fold and seal the finished empanada. In order to make things easier, it is more typical of people in Latin American countries to use a Tortilla press such as the one in the photograph below. These are quick and easy to use as well as giving the ability to produce regular shaped empanada discs every time. A tortilla press will produce empanada discs that are about 6 inches in diameter.

### An aluminium tortilla press

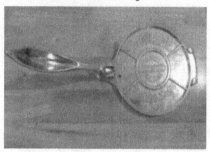

Tortilla presses can be obtained at different price levels but they all do the same basic job. The most expensive are made from cast iron and the least expensive from aluminium. The one in the image above is made from aluminium. You can easily obtain them online from Amazon or EBay.

The same technique using plastic sheets or bags is employed when using a Tortilla press. First place a plastic bag or plastic sheet on the base plate of the tortilla press. Next put a ball of empanada dough in the centre.

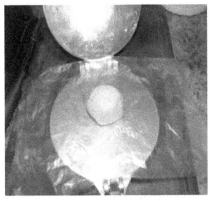

Place another sandwich bag over the top of the dough ball.

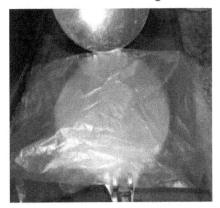

Close the press and gently press together using the lever of the tortilla press. Once you see the dough being squeezed out between the plates of the press stop and open up the press.

Transfer your disc with the plastic still round it to your work surface until it is needed. To stuff the empanada disc, first gently remove the top plastic sheet. Add a small amount of your filling to the centre of the disc which is still supported by the lower plastic sheet.

Using the bottom plastic sheet for support, fold the whole thing so that the edges of the empanada disc meet. Squeeze these together to form the seal.

When you are ready to fry the empanada gently peel away the plastic sheet so that the empanada can be placed in the frying pan or deep frying basket. Do this carefully so that the plastic comes away from the empanada without ripping its surface.

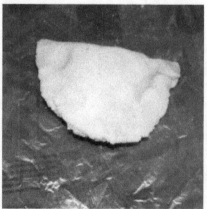

It is best to use fresh plastic sheets for each empanada that you make so that the dough doesn't stick to the surface of the plastic. If you reuse the bags over again you should make sure that they are cleaned and dried.

## Frying the empanada

Empanada can be fried in a variety of oils but good results are obtained when oils such as sunflower, canola or peanut are used.

A deep fat fryer can be used or even just a deep frying pan. Set the deep fat fryer to 175 to 180c (350 to 365F). Smaller empanada cook more quickly and benefit from a temperature in the lower range. Don't put too many empanada in the frying basket as they may stick together. You will need to turn the empanada over half way through cooking so that both sides cook and become a nice golden brown colour.

When using a frying pan ensure that the oil is deep enough to cover at least half of the empanada depth. This means that when they are turned the empanadas are completely cooked. The oil will be hot enough when it bubbles when the empanada is placed in it. Fry the first side until it is golden brown and then turn to do the other side. Make sure that you don't put too many in the pan at the same time as they will tend to stick together and then break up. If any do start to leak their contents remove them from the pan. Once an empanada is cooked on both sides, remove it from the pan and place it on a paper towel to allow the excess oil to drain away. Serve the fried empanada while they are still nice and warm

A batch of small deep fried empanada

# Empanada recipes from around the world

Empanada dough and fillings are made differently in various countries of the world. Here are some example recipes that you can try in order to experience some of these different flavours and textures. Each country has its own way of doing things and uses their own local ingredients such as spices and herbs to produce exciting and unique styles of empanada. Where there may be difficulty obtaining certain ingredients alternatives have been suggested to use instead. Here are some recipes that are typical of the areas around the world that they originate:

# Argentina

## Beef empanadas

### Ingredients

To make about 10 empanadas

### Filling
2 tablespoon extra-virgin olive oil
1 medium onion
2 garlic cloves
2 tablespoon chopped green onion
1 red bell pepper
450g ground beef
10 pitted green olives
1 teaspoon paprika
½ teaspoon cumin
2 hardboiled eggs
salt and pepper to taste

**Dough**
300g plain flour
120g cold salted butter, cut into ½-inch cubes
1 large egg
80ml ice cold water
1 tablespoon vinegar

**Cooking**
Sunflower oil for frying

**Method**

Chop the onion. Mince the garlic. Remove the seeds from the red pepper and then cut it up into small chunks. Finely chop the olives. Roughly chop the boiled eggs.

Put the olive oil into a large frying pan and put it on a medium heat. Once the oil is hot fry the onions and garlic for a few minutes until the onion becomes translucent. Add the chopped green onion and the red pepper to the pan and fry for a few more minutes. Break up the mince beef and add it to the pan. Continue to fry the beef and once it is browned season with salt and pepper to taste. Next, stir in the olives, boiled egg, cumin and paprika and cook until the mixture is no longer runny.

**Cooked filling**

Turn off the heat and allow the mixture to cool before placing it in the fridge for a few hours before it is used for the empanada filling.

The dough is made by the same methods as detailed in the first section. The only extra ingredient is the white vinegar which can be added and whisked with the egg before adding to the mixture. Once the dough has cooled in the fridge divide it up into ten equally sized portions about the size of a golf ball.

**10 dough balls ready for rolling out into discs**

Roll each dough ball out to form a disc that is about 3mm thick. Put filling in the centre of each disc and fold to form the empanada. Use a fork to press the edges together to make a better seal.

These empanada are best fried. Once the oil is hot, fry each side for a couple of minutes until each is golden brown. Put the cooked empanadas on a paper towel to drain off the excess oil and the serve while they are still hot.

**Some fried beef empanada**

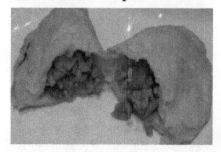

The filling inside the cooked empanada

# Belize
## Fish panada

The people of Belize have a great love of spicy food as well as fish. In Belize they call empanadas panadas but essentially they are a fried form of empanadas. This next recipe is a popular fish panada that is often made there.

### Ingredients
### The filling
2 cans of tuna in water (185g)
Small bunch of fresh coriander
2 green or red chiilies
1 medium onion
Black pepper and salt

### The dough
500g of masa dough made from PAN precooked corn meal or masa harina
1 tsp baking powder
½ tsp paprika pepper (You can use Recado spice if you have it)

### Panada sauce
1 large onion
½ cabbage
1 chilli
Freshly ground black pepper
100ml water
100ml vinegar

### Method
Chop the coriander, chillies and the onion.

Open the canned tuna and then spoon the tuna meat into a medium sized pan. Break the tuna meat up in the pan and then add the chopped coriander, chillies and onion. Stir the mixture in the pan and then place on a medium heat. Cook the tuna until the remaining tuna liquid is driven off and the overall mixture appears dry but don't allow it to burn. Add black pepper and salt to taste. Don't add salt if your canned tuna already contains salt.

Make up the masa dough by mixing the dry ingredients together as detailed on the dry flour pack. Add the baking powder and paprika as dry ingredients to the flour before you add any water to the mix. Take the smooth dough and then mix in the baking powder and the paprika. Roll the dough mixture into a large ball and then pinch off pieces to roll in your hands. You should aim for each one to be about the size and shape of a golf ball.

Use the tortilla press with the dough balls between plastic to press out each panada disc. You can use a rolling pin and board if you don't have a press.

Spoon the tuna filling into the centre of each panada disc and then fold and seal them.

Shallow fry or deep fry the panada depending on your preference. In Belize they usually use shallow frying in a large pan. Put the pan on a medium heat. Take care not to have the oil too hot as the panada will cook too quickly leaving the inside cold and the outside will possibly burn. The oil should bubble in a relatively calm way when the panada are frying. If the outside of the panada forms large blisters then the oil is too hot. Cook each side until they are golden in colour. Put the cooked panadas on paper towel to drain away the excess oil.

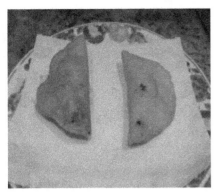

To make the panada sauce chop the onion and shred the cabbage. Chop the chilli pepper. Add the mixture to a serving bowl and add some freshly ground black pepper to taste. Add the water and vinegar and stir to mix everything together.

Serve the panadas while they are still warm and cover them with the sauce.

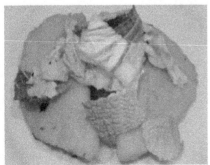

# Columbia
## Pork and beef empanada

These pork and beef empanada are served with limes and a special Columbian hot sauce called Aji. The recipe here will produce around 20 delicious empanadas.

### Ingredients

**Aji sauce and garnish**
1 small hot chilli pepper
120ml vinegar
60ml water
¼ teaspoon salt
1 teaspoon sugar
1 tablespoon lime juice
2 tablespoon extra virgin olive oil
1 handful fresh coriander leaves
1/2 handful fresh parsley
2 or 3 green spring onion
1 tomato

Chopped limes for garnish

**Sazon spice mix**
½ teaspoon ground coriander seeds
½ teaspoon ground cumin
½ teaspoon ground paprika
½ teaspoon garlic powder

½ teaspoon salt

## Empanada dough
1 ½ cups precooked cornmeal (PAN)
1 ½ cups water
1 tablespoon extra virgin olive oil
½ tablespoon Sazon spice mix
½ teaspoon Salt

## Filling
450g peeled and diced white potatoes
1 vegetable stock cube
1 tablespoon extra-virgin olive oil
1 small white onion
2 tomatoes
½ teaspoon sea salt
2 green spring onions
1 garlic clove
2 tablespoon chopped fresh coriander leaves
1 small red bell pepper
¼ teaspoon black pepper
250g ground pork and beef

## Method

### Aji sauce

Spirit white vinegar is typically used, but you can use other vinegars just the same. I tend to use raw apple cider vinegar. You can leave out the sugar and salt if you need to avoid these.

Deseed the chilli pepper. Put the pepper, water and vinegar into a blender and whiz up for a couple of minutes.

Chop the parsley, coriander, tomato and spring onion and put them into a mixing bowl. Add the lime juice and the olive oil together with the salt and sugar, if needed. Add the vinegar water and pepper mixture and stir everything so that it is well combined. Transfer to a suitable storage jar. The Aji will keep in the fridge for up to about 2 weeks.

### Sazon spice mix

If you have access to the readymade Sazon spice mix, that you can buy, then use that as it will contain all the correct local ingredients. If it is not available in your area you can make up the following version using commonly available spices. Only half a teaspoon is needed in the recipe, but in order to mix the correct proportions of reach spice you will end up making more than this. The extra spice mix can be kept in an air tight container until needed in the future.

Simply mix the spices listed in the ingredients together so that they are well combined. Leave out the salt if you do not want it.

### Empanada dough

Put the precooked cornmeal into a mixing bowl and then stir in the salt and Sazon spice mix dry ingredients. Mix so that everything is combined well. Use a rubber spatula to stir the mixture as you add the olive oil and water. As the dough comes together shape it into a ball with your hands. Knead the dough for a few minutes until it becomes nice and smooth. You can use the dough to make discs after the dough has stood for about 5 minutes.

### Filling

Dissolve the stock cube in hot water and then use it to boil the potatoes in a saucepan until they are tender. Drain off the remaining liquid and then mash the cooked potatoes. Save the mash for use later.

Chop the white onion, tomatoes, spring onion, garlic and bell pepper.

Heat the olive oil in a large frying pan and then add the chopped white onion. Cook until the onion becomes translucent. Next add the spring onion, tomato, bell pepper, coriander, garlic, black pepper and salt. Stir the mixture and cook on a medium heat for around fifteen minutes.

Add the pork and beef to the pan and stir to break up any lumps of meat as it cooks. Once the meat has browned and the pan contents appear quite dry pour the mixture into the bowl with the mashed potato. Stir the contents of the bowl until the mashed potato is well mixed with the fried ingredients. Leave the combined mixture to cool.

**Preparing the empanada**

Roll the dough into small balls about the size of a golf ball using your hands. Produce dough discs by either using the taco press or rolling out between pieces of clean plastic. See the previous section for details. Place filling in the centre of each disc and then fold and seal the edges of the empanada using a fork.

Deep fry or shallow fry the empanada in vegetable oil. Place each newly cooked empanada on paper towels to soak up the excess oil.

Serve the empanadas with cut limes and the Aji sauce.

# Chile

## Pino empanada

Pino describes the special Chilean filling used in these empanada. It uses chunks of beef rather than the usual minced beef used in other areas of Latin America. The filling is well seasoned and often contains raisins, hard boiled eggs and black olives. The following recipe makes 10 empanadas.

### Ingredients

**Pino filling**
2 tablespoons olive oil
500g chopped beef
½ teaspoon paprika
½ teaspoon dried oregano
½ teaspoon cumin
1 teaspoon salt
Freshly ground black pepper
½ cup water
1 large onion chopped
1 tablespoon plain flour

20 black olives
About 30 raisins
2 boiled eggs

**Dough**

½ cup milk
½ cup warm water
2 teaspoon salt
450g plain flour
2 egg yolks
80g melted butter
Egg wash

**Method**

**Pino filling**

Put the olive oil into a large frying pan and place it onto a medium heat. Add the meat to the pan and cook, while stirring, until the beef is browned. Stir in the cumin, oregano, paprika, salt and ground pepper. After everything is well mixed add the chopped onion and water. Once the mixture is simmering turn down the heat to low and continue to cook for about a half an hour. After cooking leave the filling to cool and then place it in the refrigerator.

**Dough**

Mix the milk, salt and water in a small bowl until the salt has dissolved.

Add the flour and egg yolks to a large mixing bowl and combine with a rubber spatula or fork. Add the butter and continue to combine everything until it starts to have a crumb like appearance. Slowly add the milk, water and salt mixture and continue to mix with the rubber spatula. Knead the dough with your hands until it is nice and soft with an elastic texture. More salt water and milk mix can be added if the dough is too dry.

Divide the dough into ten pieces the same size and roll each up into a ball. Use a rolling pin on each ball of dough to produce discs that are about 8 inches in diameter.

**Putting it all together**

In the centre of each disc put 2 tablespoons of the pino filling and ¼ boiled egg, 2 olives and some raisins. Seal the empanada using some of the egg wash. Once sealed use a pastry brush to cover the surface of the empanadas with more egg wash.

Place the empanadas on a baking sheet and place in a preheated oven set to 180C. Bake for about thirty minutes or until they are a nice golden brown colour. Serve the empanadas while they are still hot.

# Indian

## Samosa

Samosas are a popular Indian snack or starter. They are typically triangular in shape. Although you can make them with meat such as lamb or chicken they are usually vegetarian in nature.

This recipe makes about 12 samosas

### Ingredients

### Dough

1 ½ cups plain flour
¾ teaspoon salt
¼ teaspoon ajwain seeds ( use thyme if not available)
2 tablespoons olive oil
1 tablespoon lemon juice
5-7 tbsp. cold water (80-100ml)

### Filling

1 teaspoon coriander seeds
1 teaspoon fennel seeds
1 ½ pounds potatoes
Salt to taste
½ teaspoon dry mango powder
½ teaspoon garam masala
½ teaspoon sugar
10 sprigs chopped coriander
½ tablespoon minced green chili
½ tablespoon minced ginger
Lime juice
2 tablespoons olive oil
½ teaspoon cumin
1/8 teaspoon asafoetida
½ cup frozen green peas

### Method

### Filling

Peel the potatoes and cut them into cubes. Boil the potatoes in a saucepan and then drain the cooking water off. Put the cooked potato in a bowl and add the coriander and fennel seeds to it. Add salt to taste. Add the mango powder, garam masala, sugar, coriander, green chili and ginger. Add some lime juice to taste. Use a spoon to mix everything up.

Put the oil into a frying pan and put on medium heat. Once hot add the cumin seeds and once sizzling add the asafoetida and green peas. Cook for a couple of minutes until they are soft and then add the potato mixture. Stir the mixture and continue to cook until everything is heated through.

## Dough

Put the flour into a mixing bowl and the stir in the salt and carrom seeds. Add the oil and then mix with your fingers until the oil is well incorporated and no lumps of oil remain. Once this is done add the lemon juice. Stir and then add the water. Knead the mixture into a soft dough. Roll the dough into a ball and cover with plastic wrap. Leave the dough to rest for about 20 minutes.

Once the dough has rested and is back to room temperature remove it from the plastic wrap and knead it a few more times. Divide your dough into portions depending on how many you want to make. Each portion will make 2 samosas.

## Rolling and stuffing

Roll out a portion of the dough using a rolling pin on a work surface. Roll it thinly into an oval shape.

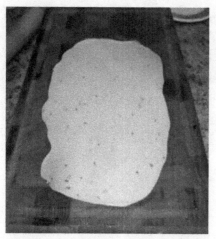

Cut the oval shape in half using a knife.

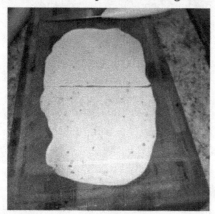

Rub some water down half of the cut edge using a finger and then fold the other half of the cut edge towards it forming a cone shape. Seal the edges by squeezing them together.

Divide the filling mixture into portions depending on how many samosas you want to make. Spoon a portion of filling into the cone shaped dough held in one hand. Try not to over stuff it as the top edges need to seal over the filling.

Rub some water round the top inner edges of the cone shaped dough and then bring them together and squeeze to seal them. Fold the seal slightly to the one side of the samosa.

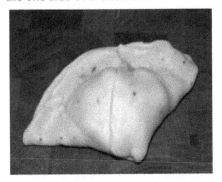

Deep fry the samosas in oil on a medium heat. Once they are golden brown remove them from the oil and place them on paper towelling to absorb the excess oil.

You can serve the samosas on their own or with tamarind and mint Indian chutney.

# Great Britain

## Cornish Pasty

**Ingredients**

**Dough**

325g Plain Flour
200g unsalted Cold Butter
120 ml Cold Water
60 ml Cold Water

**Filling**

2 tablespoons olive oil
450g diced stewing steak
450g diced peeled potato
250g diced turnip

250g chopped onion
Salt and freshly ground black pepper to taste
Egg wash

**Method**

Use the method described in the Flakier and Tastier Empanada dough section to produce the dough. The ingredients above are the same as in that section.

Put the diced potato and turnip into a pan of water and boil until the potato is cooked but the cubes still remain in shape. This should take about 15 minutes. Drain the water and save the turnip and potato for later

Put the olive oil into a large frying pan and place on a medium heat. Fry the onion until it is translucent and then add the steak. Continue to fry until the meat is nice and browned. Season with salt and pepper to taste. Once cooked turn off the heat and add the part cooked turnip and potato to the pan. Stir so that all of the ingredients are combined. Save this for filling the pasty.

Roll out the dough in the normal way and cut discs of the size that you want. You can make any size that you wish but I often make large ones so that they can be shared between a number of people.

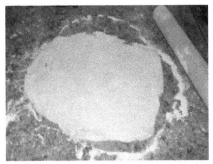

Place a suitable amount of filling in the centre of each disc and then fold in the normal way and seal the edges using the help of some of the egg wash. With large pasties it is easy to fold over the sealed edges to make them more secure.

Coat each pasty with egg wash and place on a baking sheet. Cook the pasties in a preheated oven set to 200C for between 20 and 30 minutes until they are golden brown in colour. Serve the cooked pasties while they are still hot. Pasties can be eaten on their own as a meal or served with French fries or boiled vegetables.

# Conclusion

The Empanada is a very versatile type of food and it seems that everywhere has its own version of this popular dish. They can be used as a simple snack or the basis for a full meal. Depending on what you put inside an empanada and the size you make, it can even become a whole meal in itself. As you have seen empanadas are great for using up leftovers, and as a result the ones that you make are always changing in their nature. This means that there are always fresh flavours to experience round the corner.

Despite the ease by which different fillings can be produced for the empanadas that you make, it is a great idea to try out recipes popular in different parts of the world.

There is a definite difference in the flavours between those that use wheat for the dough and those that use corn masa. Make sure that you try both out. There is also a considerable difference between frying and baking the empanadas. Try both. I prefer the baked method but for some types such as Indian samosas and those made from corn dough frying is the way to go.

This book contains the recipes for empanadas from a small number of different countries. There are still many other countries that have their own special empanada recipes. Look out for recipes from countries such as Indonesia, Spain, Goa, Italy and the Philippines. Even within the same country there are differences between regions. For example, in this book the Indian recipe is given for the savoury samosa. In other regions such as those in Northern India the empanada are very different and are mainly sweet in nature using ingredients such as dried fruits, nuts and dried coconut. Look out for recipes from different countries and regions and try them out. They will all add to your mastery of the humble empanada.

## About the Author

Elisabetta Parisi has written several other books including some specializing in various recipes from the Mediterranean region including her home country Italy. Here are the details of some of the other books that you can buy.

Homemade Pasta Dough

Making your own pasta is a very satisfying way to spend your time in the kitchen. The rewards come from both the effort that you put in and the fantastic new tastes that you can create for your family and friends at meal time.

Homemade Pasta Dough explains how to make many different kinds of pasta from the raw ingredients. The book explains how to make pasta dough both by hand and using various machines to help cut down the work involved.

Fresh pasta made at home is a very healthy option and there are lots of ways that you can vary the pasta dough you make. This will then add life to your pasta meals. The book contains details of mixing, rolling, cutting, stuffing and shaping your pasta.

This is an updated and extended version of the original popular book with lots of new pasta dough recipes which will extend your pasta repertoire. There are also more details on stuffed pastas such as ravioli and tortellini as well as dessert style pasta. Also now included, are example recipes showing where the different pasta doughs and shapes can be used.

www.ingramcontent.com/pod-product-compliance
Lightning Source LLC
LaVergne TN
LVHW092338040225
802993LV00028B/576